DATE DUE

MAY 0 2 2005	
FEB 09 09	JUL 26 '07
JAN 29 '11	JAN 14 '19

DEMCO, INC. 38-2931

YANKTON COMMUNITY LIBRARY

FAMOUS NATIVE AMERICAN LEADERS

THE LIGHT-HAIRED ONE
The story of Crazy Horse

Written by: Jill C. Wheeler
Edited by: Paul J. Deegan

Published by Abdo & Daughters, 6537 Cecilia Circle, Bloomington, Minnesota 55435

Library bound edition distributed by Rockbottom Books, Pentagon Tower, P.O. Box 36036, Minneapolis, Minnesota 55435

Copyright© 1989 by Abdo Consulting Group, Inc., Pentagon Tower, P.O. Box 36036, Minneapolis, Minnesota 55435. International copyrights reserved in all countries. No part of this book may be reproduced in any form without written permission from the publisher. Printed in the United States.

Library of Congress Number: 89-084913   ISBN: 0-939179-66-0

Cover Photo by: Bettmann Archive
Illustrations by: Liz Dodson

"The blue coats are coming!"

At the sound of the cry, Curly put down the rawhide-covered club he had been making and turned to see what was causing the excitement. The young boy was visiting the village of his mother. He had not heard about any hunting parties coming back that day.

All around the Brule village, people stared at the Holy Road. The Holy Road was a narrow, dusty track. It led from the white man's fort. The whites used it to travel west through the land of the Sioux. Now, a giant dust cloud hovered over the road as a long column of blue-coated soldiers tramped toward the Indian camp. At the rear of the column were two wagons loaded with huge guns, their giant barrels glistened in the sunlight.

"Why do they come?" Curly asked his friend He Dog, who was visiting the Brule village, too. "Why do they not leave us alone as they promised?"

"It is about the cow," He Dog explained.

"The cow?"

"Yes, that skinny old cow Straight Foretop the Minneconjou killed after it ran through our camp," He Dog added.

"Oh yes," Curly said. "I remember. The poor animal was no good to eat. I don't know why the white man who owned it ever thought it would make it across the mountains. Did not our people offer to give the man a good horse in exchange?"

"They offered *five* good horses, and they did not even say *anything* about the white man paying for the damage his cow did when it tore our tipis and tipped over our cooking pots," He Dog said bitterly. "The white man only wants to make trouble, and it looks like he has."

The two boys walked closer to where the blue coats had stopped. Chief Conquering Bear had walked out to meet them. Many warriors gathered to hear their chief ask for a peaceful solution.

"We have come to arrest the Minneconjou," the soldier's leader said. "He must come with us to the fort and face trial."

Straight Foretop had been standing quietly behind Conquering Bear. Straight Foretop's gun was cradled lightly in his arms. He listened as the interpreter translated the soldier's words, then he stepped forward.

"The whites have already killed all of my family," he said bravely. "There is only me now, and I will not go alive."

The interpreter began his translation, but he twisted the words, causing the soldier's chief to become very angry. Suddenly, the white chief lifted his hand and the guns of the whites began to boom. Chief Conquering Bear fell to the ground as a bullet ripped through his middle. The huge guns on the wagons also began to explode, sending shells tearing through the tipis in the village.

At the sight of the fallen chief, the warriors who had gathered raised their bows and began to shoot into the blue coats' ranks. Within minutes, most of the white soldiers lay dead, and those near the back of the column were running toward the fort with a crowd of angry Brules close behind. Soon all the whites had been killed, as well as many Indians. Among the dead was the sly interpreter who had twisted Conquering Bear's words to anger the white soldiers.

Curly and He Dog climbed on to their horses and began to ride back to their village, leaving the stench of blood and gunsmoke behind. The white soldiers were gone, but the troubles with the whites had only just begun.

The next few days were anxious ones in the Oglala camp where Curly lived with his father and step mother. The young warriors in the camp were bound by tradition to avenge the death of their leader. If they did not, the relatives of the fallen chief would be disgraced.

One morning, Curly watched the warriors ride out of the village in their war paint. They sang war songs. He wished he could go with them. But he was only 12 snows old. Also, his father, Crazy Horse, was a medicine man, not a warrior or a chief. Most warriors were sons of warriors.

Later, the band of fighters returned. The tribe gathered around the campfire to hear what had happened. The fighters had ambushed a white man's mail coach on the Holy Road. They had killed the driver and his companions. They had taken the three horses. They also took a worthless box of the white man's green paper and battered coins. Conquering Bear's death had been avenged.

The tribe gathered around the campfire to hear the warriors stories.

Man Afraid, the new chief, then made an announcement. The tribe would be moving back to their sacred hunting ground. They would return to the Black Hills of modern-day South Dakota for the winter.

That winter was one of the happiest Curly had ever known. The woods were plentiful with game, and the people soon forgot the white man's cloth and tools and instead used the gifts of the Great Spirit to make their clothing and utensils.

Curly spent many hours alone in the mystic forests. He was used to being alone. He often chose solitude to escape the teasing of the other Indian boys.

Curly did not look like the other boys. He had received his name because of his hair, which was light brown and curly. The other boys' had straight, shining black locks. And Curly's skin was lighter, more like that of the white man. Curly knew some of the whites thought he was a captive or half-breed, but his father long ago had told him that the people in his family had been light-skinned throughout the ages.

To overcome his appearance, Curly had learned to excel at horse riding. He was now one of the best riders in the camp, and he hoped someday to become a great warrior. He also someday hoped to be a leader among his people, but he had competition in that area from another Indian boy, No Water. No Water was stronger and bigger than the slender Curly. No Water bragged about his deeds. Curly said nothing.

One day in the Moon of Calves Growing Hair, Curly was returning to the camp of his mother. He had just cleared the rise near the village when the storm which had been building all afternoon broke in full intensity. Through the occasional flashes of lightning, he saw the ruins of the village, still smoldering in the afternoon heat. Here and there were scattered remnants of the tribe's possessions, with some forming a trail along the creek.

A strangled cry escaped from Curly's lips as he realized some of the bundles on the ground were people. Jumping down from his horse, he ran to the village, winding his way between the bodies and fearing what he might see.

There was no one left alive in the Brule camp. "I will kill them for what they have done here today," he said softly, his fists clenched in anger. "I will kill and kill until the white man no longer roams the plains."

The storm continued to build as Curly remounted his horse. He went off in search of the soldiers who had attacked Little Thunder's camp. He moved slowly through the bloodied mess, peering into the darkness to make out faces. A sudden flash of lightning illuminated a face below him which he recognized — she had been a member of his people. *This* was what was left of his people! In despair he dropped to his knees and was sick, holding his stomach and finally falling to the ground as all went black.

He was on a great stallion which reared and pawed the air as it danced to the rumbling thunder. He and the horse seemed to float through the air over the waving grass. The blue coats were there — all around him their firesticks

Curly rides his stallion through the storm.

11

flaring and cannons roaring, crumbling tipis like the leaves of the cottonwood. He rode through the fire and the flames, beckoning to his people to follow. They tried to hold him back, but he shook them off and continued. Overhead, a red hawk circled and cryed out to the figure below in the white buckskin shirt with the small brown stone tied behind his ear. The boy turned to look at his people, but they were now lying on the ground dead, just like...

Curly sat upright suddenly. The vision! He'd had that vision before, only then he did not know what it meant. But here, sitting among the torn and mutilated bodies heavy with the smell of death, he understood its meaning. He must lead his people against the whites. That was what the Great Spirit intended for him to do.

And do it he would.

Curly's tribe was moving to the Big Horn Mountains. The name came from the majestic big horn goats who climbed them so effortlessly.

One day, in the new camp, Curly felt someone's gaze upon him. Glancing up, he caught the eye of Black Buffalo Woman, the niece of the great chief Red Cloud. Discovered, the girl turned away, but Curly did not forget her soft brown gaze.

He had known the girl ever since she was a baby, and she recently had become a woman in the Sioux tradition with a feast in her honor. Now she was eligible to be married. Curly would have liked to marry her, but knew he must concentrate on carrying out those tasks the Great Spirit had shown him in his vision.

Steeling his mind to the tasks before him, he stood up gracefully and went to prepare to join a war party against the Crows. Suddenly, as he walked towards his tipi, a bolt of pain shot through his knee, and he looked down to see he had been struck by an arrow. His father, who had seen him stumble, came running from their tipi.

"My son! You have been hurt," he said, gently cradling the injured knee in his large hands. Despite the pain, Curly did not make a sound as his father removed the arrow and held it up for him to see.

"It is an Oglala arrow," Crazy Horse said solemnly. "The vision is coming true. Your own people are the only ones who can hold you back. Do you know who did this?" he asked.

"No," Curly said. "I did not see."

"You will have to be careful," Crazy Horse said slowly, staring earnestly into his son's eyes. "Your powers are great, and some are afraid of you. They resent what the Great Spirit has chosen you to do."

With the help of his father, Curly's knee healed quickly, and he once again joined his friends and the other warriors in the tribe on their hunting and scouting parties. It was after one successful raid on a band of Snake Indians that he received his adult name, Crazy Horse. His father announced the honor by walking through the village, and later there was a feast and dancing to celebrate the tribe's newest warrior.

One day, in the new camp, Curly felt someone's gaze upon him. Glancing up, he caught the eye of Black Buffalo Woman, the niece of the great chief Red Cloud. Discovered, the girl turned away, but Curly did not forget her soft brown gaze.

He had known the girl ever since she was a baby, and she recently had become a woman in the Sioux tradition with a feast in her honor. Now she was eligible to be married. Curly would have liked to marry her, but knew he must concentrate on carrying out those tasks the Great Spirit had shown him in his vision.

Steeling his mind to the tasks before him, he stood up gracefully and went to prepare to join a war party against the Crows. Suddenly, as he walked towards his tipi, a bolt of pain shot through his knee, and he looked down to see he had been struck by an arrow. His father, who had seen him stumble, came running from their tipi.

"My son! You have been hurt," he said, gently cradling the injured knee in his large hands. Despite the pain, Curly did not make a sound as his father removed the arrow and held it up for him to see.

"It is an Oglala arrow," Crazy Horse said solemnly. "The vision is coming true. Your own people are the only ones who can hold you back. Do you know who did this?" he asked.

"No," Curly said. "I did not see."

"You will have to be careful," Crazy Horse said slowly, staring earnestly into his son's eyes. "Your powers are great, and some are afraid of you. They resent what the Great Spirit has chosen you to do."

With the help of his father, Curly's knee healed quickly, and he once again joined his friends and the other warriors in the tribe on their hunting and scouting parties. It was after one successful raid on a band of Snake Indians that he received his adult name, Crazy Horse. His father announced the honor by walking through the village, and later there was a feast and dancing to celebrate the tribe's newest warrior.

One day, Crazy Horse noticed that Black Buffalo Woman was looking at him in a new way. She no longer seemed shy. Her looks were those of admiration and friendship.

He came across her alone, another day while she was picking berries nearby. In the custom of the tribe, he swung his blanket around her, pulling her close and asking her about her family. She replied quietly, but he scarcely heard her answer so loudly was his heart pounding. He had noticed that No Water also was taking an interest in the young woman, but Black Buffalo Woman only ignored him.

Word soon came that the chief Red Cloud was organizing a party against the Crows. Crazy Horse was quickly picked to join them, as his bravery was well known. This time, his younger brother, Little Hawk, also was chosen to go. Crazy Water was privately glad that No Water complained of a toothache and said he couldn't go along.

The party traveled for several days over rocky foothills and barren plains until they came to the Crow camp. It was nestled in a small valley. Crazy Horse's party waited until the next day.

Every brave knew battle at night was not good. When dawn broke, the attack began.

Crazy Horse and the other warriors charged down into the valley, whooping and screaming as they urged their horses faster and faster. The startled Crows barely had time to wake up.

Crazy Horse was excited. He was one of the best horsemen in the village, and now was one of the times it was an advantage. He slid to one side of his mount, riding so low only his eyes were visible as they peered over the horse's back. From that position, he could shoot safely.

Circling the camp, Crazy Horse sought the tipi of the chief. It was the one in the center of the camp. It had the most stories of coup and bravery painted on it. He picked it out, and as he watched it the chief stumbled out. The chief still was fumbling with his heavily beaded moccasins.

Closing one eye, Crazy Horse aimed and fired. A blast of crimson spread across the chief's chest as he fell to the ground. Crazy Horse whooped a victory cry. He sped off to join the rest of the war party as they made their retreat.

He had killed an enemy chief! The coups and the honors would be his tonight.

The war party was still several miles from camp when they were met by a greeting party. The warriors spoke excitedly about their victories as the greeters told what happened while they were gone.

Crazy Horse was rubbing down his horse while the rest of the warriors chattered away. He overheard snatches of the conversation, and did not even smile when he heard his name mentioned along with the many brave things he had done.

"...killed the chief! The Crow did not even die with his moccasins on!" he heard another warrior saying.

"...is seeking the vision. He will return to camp this evening and have the vision interpreted..." said one of the greeting party.

"...Black Buffalo Woman..."

Crazy Horse froze at the mention of Black Buffalo Woman. He stopped working and strained his ears to hear what was being said.

"...is in the lodge of No Water now. He will bring power to her family."

Crazy Horse felt the blood drain from his face. The sky above seemed to begin swirling. The voices behind him dissolved into the howling of the wind. Black Buffalo Woman had married another while he was away! And she had married No Water — his rival!

The next few days passed in a haze. Crazy Horse wanted neither company nor sympathy. He spent his time alone in his lodge or out in the wilderness. Finally he went off alone, back to the land of the Crows. He returned with scalps and guns, and life went on.

Shortly after his journey, he was returning from a hunt when he saw her alone gathering herbs in the woods. She tried to hide from him, but he only stopped near her and stared silently.

"It was my duty to my family to marry No Water," she said finally.

"I do not hate you. I can never hate you," Crazy Horse said softly, and then turned his mount and urged it back to camp, leaving the young woman behind, staring at his rigid back.

Devil's Tower in Wyoming, is one of the Sioux Indians most important natural monuments.

The whites were becoming more and more bold. Now one, called Bozeman, was working his way through the Sioux's finest hunting grounds toward the Powder River. As he went, he left sticks in the ground. At first the Indians did not realize the purpose of the sticks, but they soon learned the sticks marked the place of another white man's road.

As more whites came along that and the other trails through the Indians' land, the buffalo grew scarce. The whites used their firesticks to shoot whole herds. They then stripped the hides, leaving the valuable meat and bones and all the other gifts of the buffalo to the wolves.

The Indians were puzzled by such waste — they used every part of their friend the buffalo. The whites only wanted the hides to send back to their people in the east. They also took the hides of the beaver, the otter and even the grizzly.

The whites also were driven to a frenzy by a yellow material they called gold. It had been the discovery of this gold in the sacred Black Hills that had started much of the trouble with the whites. Now the gold had been discovered farther to the west and the whites tramped through the best Lakota hunting grounds to get to it.

The Powder River Region was the Sioux's most fertile hunting grounds.

For a time, Crazy Horse had been able to forget the whites. He forgot the pain they had caused him and his people. Hunting was still good. The plains were still alive with the bounty of the Great Spirit. Many Indians still roamed freely.

But then came bad news. The whites had massacred a band of Cheyenne on a reservation called Sand Creek. The whites had spared no one — women and children lay in pools of blood along with warriors and chiefs. The whites had mutilated the bodies and taken scalps. They had swung the scalps around in front of their fellow soldiers as they boasted of their kills.

The anger within Crazy Horse continued to smolder. It nearly burst into flames when he heard that Yellow Woman was one of the victims. He had rescued her after the Battle of the Blue Water.

"There can be no peace inside me until the whites are gone," Crazy Horse said to himself after he heard the news. "I will fight until they are gone or I am dead. And if my death is necessary, so be it."

For the next few years, he arranged and helped lead war parties on white settlers and travelers. The random, lightning strikes earned him much praise for his bravery and reinforced a theory he had held for many moons.

The whites, Crazy Horse had noticed, fought as one body, under one leader. With all their might concentrated on a single purpose, they were able to accomplish many deeds. Crazy Horse began to mention this to the other leaders, suggesting that the Lakota might learn from such tactics.

"We must fight together, as one," he told a group of warriors one day. "The old way of fighting for coups and personal honors will not work with the whites."

Despite Crazy Horse's raids, the white invasion of the Big Horns along the Bozeman Trail and Powder River had continued. The Sioux nation gathered once more. It was known now that new medicine was needed.

That medicine came in the form of an ancient society their forefathers had called upon in another time of war. It used seven older leaders, called Big Bellies, and four strong young men, the shirt-wearers, to lead the people.

Crazy Horse, to his surprise, was chosen a shirt-wearer. A tribal leader talked to the new young leaders. "It is your duty to uphold the rights of these people," he said.

"Let there be no violence, no injustice and no disorder. Man alone can live as he wishes. Men living together must follow the laws of old or fly away on the wind as a leaf from a tree."

"Man's passions can destroy him, but only if he lets go of the wisdom of ages. Keep the laws of the people and your strength shall multiply."

"Hou!" the crowd cried in agreement. they murmured excitedly as the cases holding the shirts were brought to the center of the lodge.

Each sparkling white shirt had been made specially for the wearer. They were made of big horn skins. The claws had been left on. There were pictures, made from colored porcupine quills, across the shoulders and along the arms. The sleeves were fringed with locks of hair. There was one for each enemy killed, each coup counted, each life saved and each horse stolen.

As the warriors put on the shirts, another old man addressed them solemnly.

"As you wear this shirt, you must think not of yourself but of others. Let insults wash over you as the rain. Protect those who have no strength of their own. Do not harbor hatred within you."

Crazy Horse still had not taken a wife. Perhaps that was why Black Buffalo Woman rode away from the lodge of No Water one night. She came to join Crazy Horse on a war party against the Crows. Crazy Horse was happy — his feelings for Black Buffalo Woman were as they had always been. He knew the custom of his tribe. A woman free to leave the lodge of her husband and go with another man if she wished.

For two days they rode together, Crazy Horse's face breaking into a smile much more often than usual as he glanced at the woman beside him. On the second night, they camped with another lodge of friends they had found, and were sitting around the fire after eating when the door to the lodge was suddenly thrown open.

"So, you are here," No Water said, raising his revolver and aiming at Crazy Horse. A shot rang out and Crazy Horse clutched his jaw where the bullet had smashed into his face. Black Buffalo Woman jumped up and ran from the lodge in terror. By the time the rest of the Indians realized what had happened, No Water had run away as well.

Many warriors sought to take the life of No Water. A warrior who could not handle his wife seeing another was not worthy of living.

Crazy Horse survived. The wound robbed him of his speech for a while. A fever racked his body for days.

In time Black Buffalo Woman went back to No Water. Peace returned. But bad feelings had been aroused. It was another crack threatening to split apart the Indians.

Not long after he had been shot, Crazy Horse heard that his brother, Little Hawk, had been killed by the whites. Crazy Horse had been stripped of his white shirt because of the trouble over Black Buffalo Woman. More than ever, he stayed to himself, preferring to deal with his pain alone.

But He Dog and another friend had decided he needed a wife, and Black Shawl agreed to be that woman. The following spring, Crazy Horse's daughter was born. She was named They-Are-Afraid-of-Her for the many strong deeds she would be sure to do.

Nearly 10 years had passed since Crazy Horse had been shot by No Water. The years had been hard. His daughter had died of the white man's coughing sickness. Hunger continued to haunt the last remnants of his people. There were times when it seemed some Indians would sell the sacred Black Hills to the whites. Crazy Horse found it hard to understand why the whites felt they had to buy land. Land was a gift from the Great Spirit. It was a gift to be shared by all, not owned by some.

As the last quarter of the century began, nearly all the remaining Indians were settled in one great camp with Crazy Horse as chief.

The camp a was joyful, busy place with many Indians meeting old friends for the first time in many moons.

Even a rumor that the white soldier called Yellow Hair was in the country could not entirely dampen spirits. Sitting Bull told of a vision he had had. He had seen hundreds of soldiers falling into the camp upside down. Then the Indians knew the medicine of their leaders was strong.

"The blue coats are coming!"

The now familiar cry rang out through the giant Indian camp. Crazy Horse stopped sharpening the arrow he had been making and darted out the door of the tipi.

On the horizon, he saw a cloud of dust rising near Sitting Bull's camp. The sound of gunfire and yelling also split the warm morning air.

"Come on!" Crazy Horse yelled to his warriors. "Sitting Bull's camp is being attacked. We must go fight. It is a good day to die."

Grabbing the hawk he wore on the side of his head and painting a lightning bolt on his cheek, Crazy Horse jumped on to his horse and thundered off to join the fight.

The camp was a blur of blue coats, gunsmoke and flying arrows. Upon seeing Crazy Horse and his band, the whites turned and fled to higher ground. The Indians started after them, but then realized another band of whites was attacking the rear of the camp across the river.

With a war cry, Crazy Horse whirled his horse around. He charged back toward his camp. He could see the women and children were fleeing in terror. As he splashed across the river, he caught sight of the leader, the one called Custer who had killed so many Indians before. Hatred surged inside him as he thought of the Indian blood spilled at the hands of the yellow-haired one.

The whites were outnumbered and out-fought. The band of standing soldiers grew smaller. The number of blue-coated bodies on the blood-stained ground mounted. When the smoke cleared, a brilliant summer sun shone on the bodies of nearly 200 white soldiers. The plains were silent once again. Crazy Horse's warriors had fought well.

"Why?" Crazy Horse asked himself as he walked among the bodies. "Why did they attack us? We were hurting no one. Why must they kill us?"

Glancing up, he saw that some of his warriors were moving toward a group of soldiers who had retreated up into the nearby hills.

"Leave them," he shouted. "The whites have fought bravely. And there has been enough death today."

Crazy Horse's heart was heavy. Black Shawl was growing sicker and sicker with the white man's coughing disease, and Crazy Horse made arrangements to ride to the Spotted Tail reservation to see the white medicine man there.

As they were climbing into the wagon to begin the journey, they were stopped by a group of Indians who worked for the whites.

He talked the leader into letting them take Black Shawl to the doctor, but the Indian soldiers followed him. They said they were taking him to see the white soldier chief and that he would not be harmed.

It was late in the evening when he was escorted in to see the white chief. But as he stepped inside the building, Crazy Horse saw that its windows were barred like a white man's jail. He ran. Outside he drew a knife. Indian soldiers grabbed him. He did not see the white soldier who thrust a bayonet into his side. Wounded, he slid to the ground, lost in a mist of pain and darkness.

He felt himself being carried inside a building and laid upon a bed. The sounds grew more and more distant as the pain ceased and Crazy Horse found a peace which he had never found in life.

The white officals were upset. Crazy Horse's body was gone from the scaffold on which it had been placed. It had been taken away in the night. The soldiers questioned Crazy Horse's family. Where was the body?

But the family was silent.

The location of Crazy Horse's grave remains a mystery to all but the prairie winds of his beloved homeland.

The Great Sioux Chief, Crazy Horse.